Basics

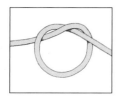

Half-hitch knot
Come out a bead and form a loop perpendicular to the thread between beads. Bring the needle under the thread away from the loop. Then go back over the thread and through the loop. Pull gently so the knot doesn't tighten prematurely.

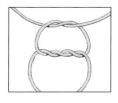

Overhand knot
Make a loop and pass the working end through it. Pull the ends to tighten the knot.

Square knot
1 Cross the left-hand cord over the right-hand cord, and then bring it under the right-hand cord from back to front. Pull it up in front so both ends are facing upward.
2 Cross right over left, forming a loop, and go through the loop, again from back to front. Pull the ends to tighten the knot.

Surgeon's knot
Cross the right end over the left and go through the loop. Go through again. Pull the ends to tighten.
Cross the left end over the right and go through once. Pull the ends to tighten.

Flattened crimp
1 Hold the crimp bead using the tip of your chainnose pliers. Squeeze the pliers firmly to flatten the crimp.
2 Tug the clasp to make sure the crimp has a solid grip on the wire. If the wire slides, remove the crimp bead and repeat the steps with a new crimp bead.

Folded crimp
1 Position the crimp bead in the notch closest to the crimping pliers' handle.
2 Separate the wires and firmly squeeze the crimp.

3 Move the crimp into the notch at the pliers' tip and hold the crimp as shown. Squeeze the crimp bead, folding it in half at the indentation.
4 Test that the folded crimp is secure.

 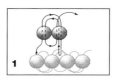

Conditioning thread
Conditioning straightens and strengthens your thread and also helps it resist fraying and tangling. Pull unwaxed nylon threads like Nymo through either beeswax (not candle wax or paraffin) or Thread Heaven to condition. Beeswax adds tackiness that is useful if you want your beadwork to fit tightly. Thread Heaven adds a static charge that causes the thread to repel itself, so it can't be used with doubled thread. All nylon threads stretch, so maintain tension on the thread as you condition it.

Stop bead
Use a stop bead to secure beads temporarily when you begin stitching. Choose a bead that is different from the beads in your project. String the stop bead about 6 in. (15cm) from the end of your thread and go back through it in the same direction. If desired, go through it one more time for added security.

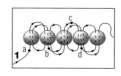

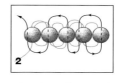

Ladder
1 Pick up two beads, leaving a 4-in. (10cm) tail. Go through both beads again in the same direction. Pull the top bead down so the beads are side by side.
The thread exits the bottom of the second bead (**a–b**). Pick up a third bead and go back through the second bead from top to bottom. Come back up the third bead (**b–c**). String a fourth bead. Go through the third bead from bottom to top and the fourth bead from top to bottom (**c–d**). Continue adding beads until you reach the desired length.
2 To stabilize the ladder, zigzag back through all the beads.

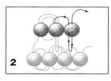

Brick stitch
Work off a stitched ladder (see Ladder).
1 Begin each brick stitch row so no thread shows on the edge: Pick up two beads. Go under the thread between the second and third beads on the ladder from back to front. Pull tight. Go up the second bead added, then down the first. Come back up the second bead.
2 For the row's remaining stitches, pick up one bead. Go under the next loop on the row below from back to front. Go back up the new bead.

Star necklace

Net a starry necklace of linked mandalas. This delicate star pattern sparkles with cut beads and crystals or semi-precious stones, but any type of seed bead will work.

Stitch the stars

[1] Pick up seven color A seed beads on a 24-in. (61cm) length of thread and slide them to 6 in. (15cm) from the end. Sew through the first bead to make a ring (**figure 1, a–b**). Pick up a 4mm bead, and sew through beads four, three, and two in the ring (**b–c**). Go through the 4mm bead again in the same direction and the remaining four beads in the ring (**c–d**).
[2] Pick up a color B seed bead and go through the next A in the ring. Repeat until you have added seven Bs, then sew through the first B (**figure 2, a–b**).
[3] Pick up a color C seed bead and go through the next B. Repeat around the ring, ending by going through the first B (**b–c**).
[4] To begin the first netting round, pick up three As and go through the next C. Repeat until there are seven three-bead sets. On the last set, end by sewing through the C and the first two As (**figure 3, a–b**).

[5] For the second round of netting, pick up five Bs and go through the middle A of the three-bead set on the previous round. Repeat around until you have made seven loops of five Bs (**b–c**). This completes a small star.

[6] Secure the thread by tying a few half-hitch knots (Basics) around the thread between beads, and trim the tail. Repeat with the other tail.

[7] To complete a large star, repeat steps 1–5. Then sew through the three Bs (**c–d**) and work one more round of netting adding seven Cs in each loop (**d–e**). End the threads as in step 6.

[8] Make eight small stars and seven large stars.

String the necklace

[1] Begin with a 2-yd. (1.8m) length of thread that has a needle on each end. Position three B beads to the center of the thread. Then bring both needles through a 4mm bead (for a button closure). Pick up a C, a bugle bead, and a C on each needle (**figure 4, a–b** and **a–c**).

[2] Bring each needle through the middle beads on two adjacent points of a small star and through the edge beads until you reach the middle beads of the two adjacent points on the other end of the star (**b–d** and **c–e**).

[3] Pick up a C, a bugle, and a C on each needle (**d–f** and **e–g**).

[4] Bring each needle through the last bead on either side of a point on a large star as shown. Weave through the edge beads until you reach first beads on either side of a point on the other side of the star (**f–h** and **g–i**).

[5] Pick up a C, a bugle, and a C on each needle (**h–j** and **i–k**).

[6] Repeat steps 2–5 until all but the last small star has been connected. Connect the last star and make a loop for the button closure as shown in **figure 5**.

– *Corrine Morris Feldman*
Corrine is a beader and glass bead maker whose work can be seen on her Web site, thegemni.com.

MATERIALS
necklace 17 in. (43cm)
- 10g size 12º 3-cut seed beads, each of **3** colors:
  color A, peach
  color B, lavender
  color C, gray
- **16** 4mm round crystals
- 5–7g 5mm bugle beads, color A
- Silamide beading thread
- beading needles, #12 or #13

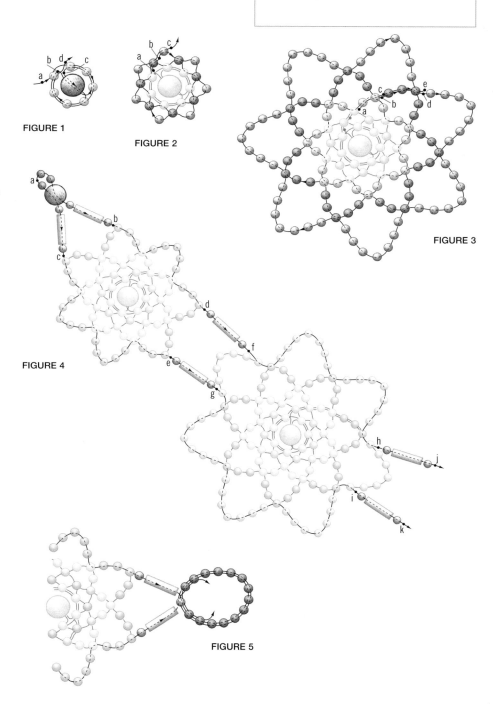

FIGURE 1

FIGURE 2

FIGURE 3

FIGURE 4

FIGURE 5

Lacy loop necklace

Use seed beads in a range of hues to create a netted collar with delicate loops. The basic pattern is easy to learn and you can alter the look by changing the color pattern or the length of the loops.

Bead the base

[1] Pick up one 11º to use as a stop bead (see Basics, p. 3) and slide it to 12 in. (30cm) from the end of a 3-yd. (2.7m) length of thread. Sew back through the bead in the same direction. Then pick up a color B 11º, three color A 11ºs, a B, three As, a B, three As, a B, and three As. Sew back through the first B strung (**figure 1, a–b**).

[2] Pick up three As, a B, three As, a B, and three As. Sew through the last B from the previous step (**b–c**).

[3] Repeat step 2 (**c–d**).

[4] Repeat until you have about 15½ in. (39.4cm) of beadwork, ending as in **figure 1, c–d**. This necklace has 39 loops along the edge of the netted base.

[5] Pick up three As, a B, and one of the soldered rings. Sew back through the B and three As. Reinforce the clasp and the last inch (2.5cm) of beadwork by retracing the thread path (**figure 2, a–b**). Secure the tails with half-hitch knots (Basics) between the beads and trim the tail. Leave the other end of the necklace unfinished in case you have to add or remove beads.

Embellish with loops

[1] Secure a new 2-yd. (1.8m) length of thread in the beadwork and exit the three As before the bottom B on the first loop (**figure 3, point a**).

[2] Pick up six As, a B, and six As. Skip the next edge B and sew through the three As before the next bottom B (**a–b**), then through the existing base beads (**b–c**). Make five loops with the same bead counts.

[3] Make the loops as in step 2, picking up seven As, a B, a teardrop bead, a B, and seven As. Make four seven-A loops.

[4] Make the loops as in step 2, picking up nine As, a B, a teardrop bead, a B, and nine As. Make four nine-A loops.

[5] Make the loops as in step 2, picking up 11 As, a B, a teardrop bead, a B, and 11 As. Make four 11-A loops.

[6] For the center of the necklace, make three loops as above, but use 15 As in the first loop, 17 in the second, and 15 in the third. Make the second half of the necklace a mirror image of the first. Secure the working thread and trim.

[7] Add a jump ring to the other end of the necklace (**figure 2, a–b**) using the tail. Attach the S-hook to the soldered rings.
– Lois Fetters

Lois is a beader who makes and sells looms with her husband, Gene. She can be contacted via e-mail at geanfet@riverview.net.

> **EDITOR'S NOTE:** Make a more dramatic necklace by switching the main and accent colors in the loops or by adding gemstones, pearls, or crystals to the loops in place of the teardrop beads.

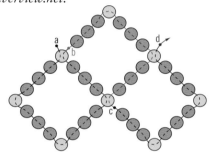

FIGURE 1

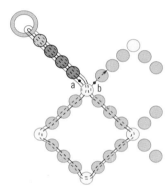

FIGURE 2

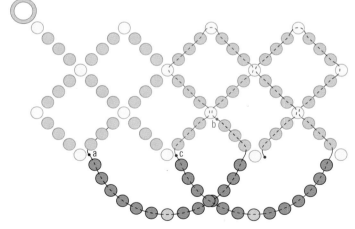

FIGURE 3

MATERIALS

necklace 16 in. (41cm)
- Japanese seed beads, size 11º
  20g color A
  10g color B
- **57** Japanese 4mm fringe or teardrop beads
- S-hook clasp with two soldered jump rings
- Silamide or conditioned Nymo D
- beading needles, #12

Sparkling black bracelet

Net an easy lace band for a sleek look.
Three-cut seed beads and faceted gemstones
give this bracelet a sophisticated edge.

MATERIALS

bracelet 6½ in. (16.5cm)
- hank size 13º seed beads, 3-cut, black
- **32 or more** 3mm faceted oval beads, jet
- clasp
- Silamide beading thread, black
- beading needle, #10 or #12

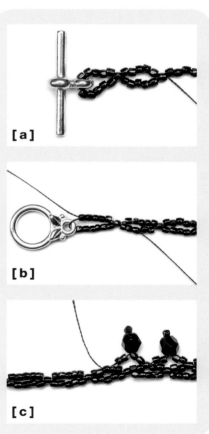

[a]

[b]

[c]

[1] Determine the finished length of your bracelet, subtract the length of the clasp, and add 10 percent to allow for shrinkage as you net the bracelet.

[2] Thread a comfortable length of Silamide on a needle. String a stop bead (see Basics, p. 3) 5 in. (13cm) from the end. String seed beads to the length determined in step 1. The number of beads strung must be divisible by six.

[3] Sew through the loop on a clasp half and pick up five seed beads. Go back though the 11th seed bead from the end. Pick up five seed beads, skip five beads on the strand, and go through the sixth bead (**photo a**).

[4] Continue along the strand, picking up five seed beads and going through the sixth seed bead until you reach the sixth seed bead from the other end. Pick up five seed beads and the other clasp half, remove the stop bead, and go through the end bead on the strand and the next seven beads to form a loop. Exit the center bead on the first net (**photo b**).

[5] Pick up two seed beads, a 3mm, and a seed bead. Skip the last seed bead and go back through the 3mm. Pick up two seed beads and go through the center bead on the next net (**photo c**).

[6] Continue adding 3mm beads along the edge of the bracelet. When you get to the end, go through the beads making the clasp loop and come out the center bead on the opposite side of the first net. Add 3mm beads to the remaining edge of the bracelet.

[7] When you reach the other end of the bracelet, go through the clasp loop again, and weave the end into the bracelet, tying a few half-hitch knots between beads. Weave in the tail the same way. Trim the ends.

– Lesley Weiss
Lesley is an Assistant Editor at Kalmbach Books.

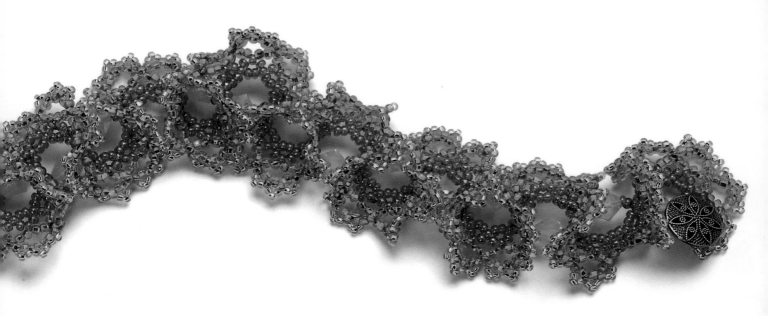

Ogalala lace bracelet

This lacy ruffled bracelet may look complex, but it's deceptively easy to master. Different shades of seed beads add dimension to the ruffles, while crystals add strength to the overall structure.

Netting

[1] Thread a needle with 1 yd. (.9m) of beading thread and string a stop bead (see Basics, p. 3) 6 in. (15cm) from the end.

[2] To allow for the take-up, or shrinkage, in the lace design, string the bracelet 25–30 percent longer than the desired finished length. To make a 6-in. (15cm) bracelet, string 9 in. (23cm) of color A seed beads. The number of beads strung must be divisible by three.

[3] Pick up three As and go through the third bead in row 1 (**figure 1, a–b**). Repeat across the entire row (**b–c**). When you reach the stop bead, remove it and knot the tail and working thread. To turn, pick up three beads and go through the center bead of the last net made on row 2 (**c–d**). Keep the tension tight as you work.

[4] Pick up five color B beads and go through the center bead of the next three-bead net (**d–e**). Work across the row as before (**e–f**). To turn, pick up five Bs and go through the center bead of the last net in row 3 (**f–g**).

[5] Pick up seven Bs and go through the center bead of the next five-bead net on the previous row (**g–h**). Repeat across the row. After you sew through the center bead on the last five-bead net, pick up seven Bs and sew through the center bead of the three-bead net on row 2 (**h–i**). Secure the thread in the beadwork and trim the tail.

Scallops

[1] Working from the center to the ends, twist and fold the lace until it forms a band with evenly scalloped edges (**photo a**). As you work, don't allow the netting to spiral around itself. The back surface of the band remains flat as you pleat the netting and form scallops on the front surface.

[2] To hold the netting in place, add seed beads and crystals between the scallops as follows: Secure the tail end of a 1 yd. length of thread near one end of the bracelet. Exit the fourth bead on row 1 (**figure 2, point a**).

[3] Pick up two 11ºs (either color), a crystal, and two 11ºs. Go through the 19th bead and work back toward the starting point, exiting at the fourth bead as before. Go through the newly strung beads and back through the 19th, 18th, 17th, and 16th beads (**a–b**).

[4] Pick up two 11ºs, a crystal, and two 11ºs. Go through the 31st bead and continue back through the beads on row 1 until you reach the 16th bead again. Go through the newly strung beads and back through the 31st, 30th, 29th, and 28th beads (**b–c**).

[5] The bead counts given for entering and exiting row 1 align with the triangular netted units made in row 2. Each scallop consists of five triangles, and the first and last triangles are shared by the neighboring scallops. To count triangles instead of individual beads from this point, work as follows: Pick up two 11ºs, a crystal, and two 11ºs as before. Count five triangles along row two starting at the 28th bead, and go through the bead that connects the fifth and sixth triangles to row 1 (**point d**). Go through the beads in the

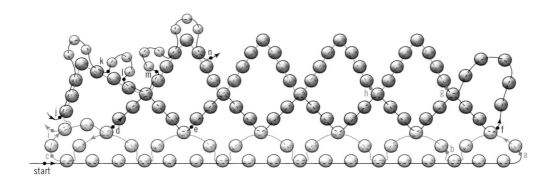

FIGURE 1

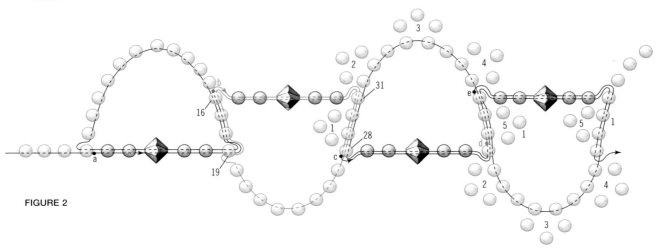

FIGURE 2

scallop you just made, back through the newly strung beads, and back through the row 1 beads in the fifth triangle. Exit through the bead that connects the fourth and fifth triangles to row 1 (**point e**). Now, string two 11ºs, a crystal, and two 11ºs as before and count five triangles from this point to make the next scallop.

[6] Continue making scallops until fewer than 16 beads remain on row 1. Secure the thread in the beadwork and trim the tails.

Picot edging

[1] Secure the thread near one end of the bracelet and exit the third bead along row 4. String three 14ºs, skip a bead, and go through the next bead along the row (**figure 1, d–k**). Repeat (**k–l**).

[2] When you reach the bead that connects the seven-bead net to the previous row, go through that bead without adding 14ºs (**k–m**), then continue adding picots on the next net (**m–n**).

[3] Repeat on the other side.

Clasp

[1] Sew a small button on one end of the bracelet.

[2] On the other end, secure a 12 in. (30cm) length of doubled thread at the edge of the beadwork. String a loop of beads just large enough to pass over the button. Go through the loop again, secure the thread in the beadwork, and cut the tails.

– Designed by Alysse Adularia
Alysse is a jewelry designer and beading instructor who owns a bead store, The Hole Affair, in Jackson, Calif. Visit her Web site, theholeaffair.com.
– Instructions by Kathy Dubuque
Kathy is an experienced beader who uses a variety of techniques. She can be reached at kdubuque@sbcglobal.net.

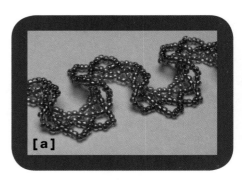

[a]

MATERIALS
bracelet 6½ in. (16.5cm)
- Japanese seed beads:
  15g size 11º in each of **2** colors, A and B
  5g size 14º, color C
- **14–16** 6mm crystal bicones
- Nymo B conditioned with beeswax or Thread Heaven
- beading needles, #12
- small button for clasp

Netted flower bracelet

Netted flowers bloom on a clever bracelet of metal snaps.

[a] [b] [c]

Bracelet assembly

[1] Cut a 24-in. (61cm) piece of beading wire. Center half the clasp on the wire. String a crimp bead, a crystal, and a crimp bead over both wire ends (**photo a**). Tighten the wires and crimp the crimp beads (see Basics, p. 3).
[2] Separate the two halves of one snap and set aside the top half. Bring both wire ends through one of the snap's holes from bottom to top (**photo b**).
[3] Separate the wires and weave each down through the next hole and up the one after that. Bring both wires down through the remaining hole (**photo c**). String a crystal or fire-polished bead

and a crimp bead over both wires, straighten out the snap so it sits evenly on the wires, and crimp the crimp bead.
[4] Continue adding snaps, crystals, and crimp beads as in step 3 until the bracelet fits comfortably around your wrist. String a crystal, a crimp bead, and the remaining clasp half on both wires. Go back through the crimp bead and crystal, tighten the loop, and crimp the crimp bead. Trim the excess wire.

Flowers

[1] On a 40-in. (1m) length of conditioned Nymo (Basics), pick up ten 8º seed beads. Go through the beads again

in the same direction and tighten them into a ring. Tie the tail and working thread together with a surgeon's knot (Basics), and go through the next bead on the ring (**figure 1, a–b**).
Round 1: Pick up three 14ºs, a color A cylinder bead, and three 14ºs. Skip the next 8º and go through the following 8º on the ring (**b–c**). Repeat, making a total of five loops (**c–d**). Go through three 14ºs, the A cylinder, and the next 14º on the first loop (**d–e**).
Round 2: Pick up three 14ºs, an A cylinder, and three 14ºs. Go through a 14º, an A cylinder, and a 14º on the second loop (**figure 2, a–b**). Repeat,

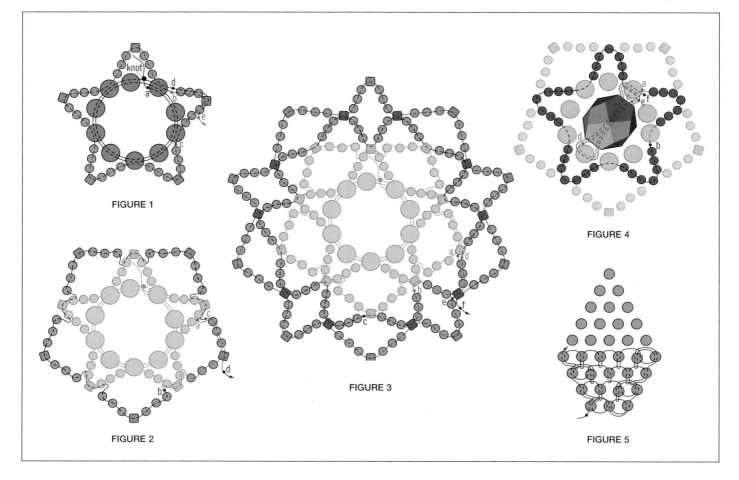

FIGURE 1

FIGURE 2

FIGURE 3

FIGURE 4

FIGURE 5

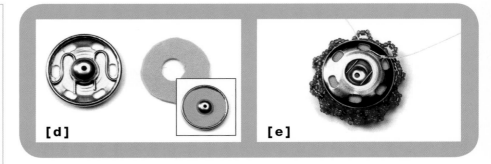

[d]

[e]

MATERIALS

bracelet 7 in. (18cm)

- **12–14** 6mm round or bicone crystals or fire-polished beads
- seed beads
  5g size 8º
  20g size 14º or 15º petal color, color A
- Japanese cylinder beads
  10g to match petal color, color A
  5g contrast color, color B
- flexible beading wire, .012
- Nymo B, conditioned with beeswax or Thread Heaven
- Illusion cord, .010
- beading needles, #12
- split needles or beading needles, #10
- **6–7** 21mm snaps (Dritz size 10)
- **8–9** crimp beads
- clasp
- 2mm-thick foam sheet (optional)
- ¼ in. (6mm) hole punch (optional)
- glue or clear nail polish
- wire cutters
- crimping pliers

EDITOR'S NOTE: There's no reason to limit your color choices when you make these netted flowers. Try stitching each layer in a different shade of one color, for example, or create your flowers in a spectrum of colors that you can arrange and rearrange whenever you like.

making a total of five loops (**b–c**). Go through three 14ºs and the A cylinder on the first loop on round 2 (**c–d**).

Round 3: Pick up three 14ºs, a B cylinder, and three 14ºs. Go through the A cylinder on round 1 (**figure 3, a–b**). Pick up three 14ºs, a B cylinder, and three 14ºs. Go through the next cylinder on round 2 (**b–c**). Repeat, making a total of ten loops (**c–d**). Go through three 14ºs, and a B cylinder (**d–e**).

Round 4: Repeat round 2 using either A or B cylinder beads. Make a total of ten loops (**e–f**). Weave through the loops to get back to the ring. (Stitch round 4 on the flower's first layer only.)

[2] For a fuller flower (like those on the green bracelet), make a second layer by repeating rounds 1–3 using 14ºs and A cylinders. Weave back to the ring.

[3] To make the next layer, repeat rounds 1–3 using B cylinders in each round. Weave back to the 8ºs on the ring.

[4] Pick up seven cylinders or 14ºs (either color), skip the next 8º on the ring, and go through the following 8º (**figure 4, a–b**). Repeat, making a total of five loops (**b–c**).

[5] With your thread exiting an 8º, pick up a crystal or fire-polished bead and go through an 8º on the opposite side of the ring (**c–d**). Go back through the crystal and the 8º (**d–e**). Repeat one more time (**e–f**). Keep the tension tight. Secure the thread and trim the tail.

[6] Make a flower for each snap on your bracelet.

Snaps

You can attach the flowers to snaps in two ways. For flowers with a higher profile (as on the green bracelet), add a layer of foam, as in steps 1 and 2 below. For a flatter look (as on the purple bracelet), sew the flowers directly onto

the snaps, as in step 3 below. Use Illusion cord with a split needle or a #10 needle for both methods.

[1] To add a layer of foam, trace the bottom half of the snap on a foam sheet. Use the hole punch to put a hole in the center of the circle. Cut out the circle, working inside the traced line (**photo d**). Press the foam into the indentation around the top of the snap (**photo d, inset**).

[2] Hold the top of the snap foam-side up and place a flower over the foam. Working from the bottom up, sew through a hole in the snap, continue through the foam, then go through a B cylinder in round 3 of the first layer. Go over the snap's edge, and tie the working thread and tail together with a surgeon's knot. Sew through the next hole and repeat (**photo e**). When you've sewn through all the snap holes and all the cylinders on round 3, knot the ends, glue the knots, and trim the tails.

[3] To attach a flower directly onto the snap, follow the sewing instructions in step 2.

Leaves (optional)

[1] Stitch a three-bead ladder (Basics) with 14ºs and conditioned Nymo, leaving a 12-in. (30cm) tail. Work the leaf in brick stitch (Basics) as shown in **figure 5**. Make one, two, or three leaves for each flower.

[2] Use the thread tail to sew the ladder beads to the center beads on the nets in round 4. Work back and forth between the ladder beads and the netting to secure the leaf.

– Linda Frechen
Linda can be reached at lfrechen@ earthlink.com.

Tubular netted necklace

Dress up a simple necklace with an embellished hollow beaded bead stitched between two netted tubes. Embellish the centerpiece as you stitch it for instant gratification.

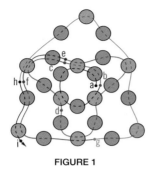

FIGURE 1

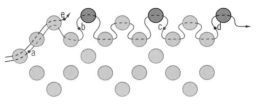

FIGURE 2

FIGURE 3

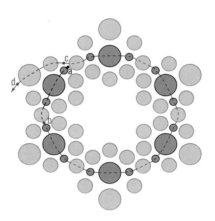

FIGURE 4

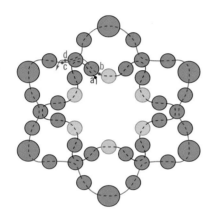

FIGURE 5

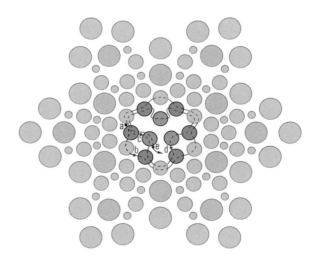

FIGURE 6

Netted tube

[1] Thread a needle with a comfortable length of Fireline. Leaving a 10-in. (25cm) tail, pick up a color A 11º seed bead and a color B 11º seed bead three times, and tie the beads into a ring with a square knot (**figure 1, a–b**). Step up through the first A and B picked up (**b–c**).

[2] Pick up an A, a B, and an A, and sew through the next B on the ring (**c–d**). Repeat twice (**d–e**), and step up through the first A and B picked up in this round (**e–f**).

[3] Work in netting stitch: Pick up an A, a B, and an A, and go through the middle bead of the next three-bead group on the previous round (**f–g**). Repeat twice (**g–h**), stepping up through the first two beads picked up in this round (**h–i**).

[4] Continue working in netting stitch for approximately 7 in. (18cm), picking up an A, a B, and an A with each stitch and going through the middle bead of the next three-bead group. Make three stitches per round.

Embellished centerpiece

[1] After making the last stitch on the first side, sew through all three beads in the next three-bead group on the last row (**figure 2, a–b**). Pick up an A, and sew through all the beads of the next three-bead group (**b–c**). Repeat (**c–d**). Pick up an A, and step up through the next A and B (**d–e**). This will result in six point beads.

[2] Work six netting stitches with As, (**figure 3, a–b**), and step up through the first two beads picked up in this round (**b–c**).

[3] Work six netting stitches, picking up an A, a 6º, and an A with each stitch (**c–d**).

[4] Working on the exterior surface, pick up a size 15º seed bead, a 4mm pearl, and a 15º, and go through the next connector bead (**figure 4, a–b** and **photo a**). Repeat around five times (**b–c**), and step up through the first A

and 6º picked up in the last round of netting (**c–d**).

[5] Work six netting stitches with 6ºs (**figure 5, a–b**).

[6] Working on the exterior, pick up a 15º, a 4mm, and a 15º, and go through the next connector bead (**b–c**). Repeat around five times (**c–d**), and step up through the first two 6ºs picked up in the last round of netting (**d–e**).

[7] Repeat steps 5 and 6, but substitute As for the 15ºs.

[8] Work six netting stitches with As. Embellish as in step 4, and step up through the first two As picked up in the last round of netting.

[9] Repeat step 8.

[10] Pick up an A, and sew through the middle bead of the next three-bead group (**figure 6, a–b**). Repeat around five times, and step up through the first A picked up in this round (**b–c**).

[11] Pick up a B, and sew through the next three As, as shown (**c–d**). Repeat around, and step up through the first B picked up in this round (**d–e**).

Finishing

[1] Resume stitching in three-bead netting stitch to make the second half of the necklace. Make the second netted tube as long as the first.

[2] To close the tube, step up through the middle bead of a three-bead group, pick up an A, and go through the middle bead of the next three-bead group. Repeat twice, and step up through the first A picked up in this round.

[3] Pick up eight to ten As and one clasp half, and sew into one of the other As in the last round (**photo b**). Retrace the thread path several times. Secure the tail with a few half-hitch knots between beads, and trim.

[4] Thread a needle on the tail at the other end, and repeat step 3.

– *Julia Gerlach*
Julia is an Associate Editor at Bead&Button *magazine.*

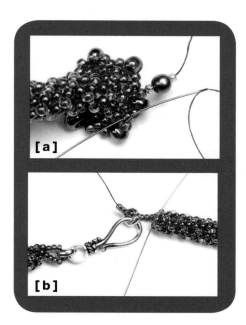

[a]

[b]

MATERIALS
necklace 16 in. (41cm)
- **30** 4mm pearls
- seed beads
  1g size 6º
  10g size 11º in each of **2** colors, A and B
- clasp
- Fireline 8-lb. test
- beading needles, #10 or #12

Ecuadorian necklace

Ecuadorian netting is woven differently from traditional netting and allows a wide variety of effects and patterns. The rainbow pattern is traditionally worn by Saraguran brides.

MATERIALS

necklace 15 in. (38cm)
- 10g size 11º seed beads in **6 or more** colors (A–F)
- bead cord, size 3 or F
- 4 yd. (3.7m) Perle cotton, #5
- Nymo D, conditioned with beeswax
- beading needles, #12
- twisted wire beading needles
- G-S Hypo Cement
- tape